Mandala Power

Color, Relax and Enjoy

COLORING BOOK FOR ADULTS AND TEENS

BY BELLA STITT

INTRODUCTION

Bella Stitt is a certified cognitive therapist who works with clients struggling with depression, anxiety and many issues related to self-esteem and self-worth. She has developed this coloring book as a coping tool to release negative feelings, thoughts or stress for those wanting an outlet or an activity to take the edge off and have a little fun.

The book is filled with mesmerizing mandalas that bring relaxation and inner peace.

Coloring, according to research, triggers and stimulates the brain areas involved with motor skills, creativity, and senses. When you color, you calm the amygdala that is located in your brain and controls both your emotions and stress/anxiety. Coloring allows you to mentally escape and take your mind off your problems—similar to what one is experiencing during meditation. In addition, it will reduce your heart rate, and increase your ability to focus.

With the pictures provided in this book, you will express your creativity with colors and discover the emotions that those colors and images will bring about. There is no right or wrong way to color or any rules to follow. You can proceed at your own pace and let yourself go by tapping into your imagination, and encouraging your self-expression and self-awareness while creating a unique work of art.

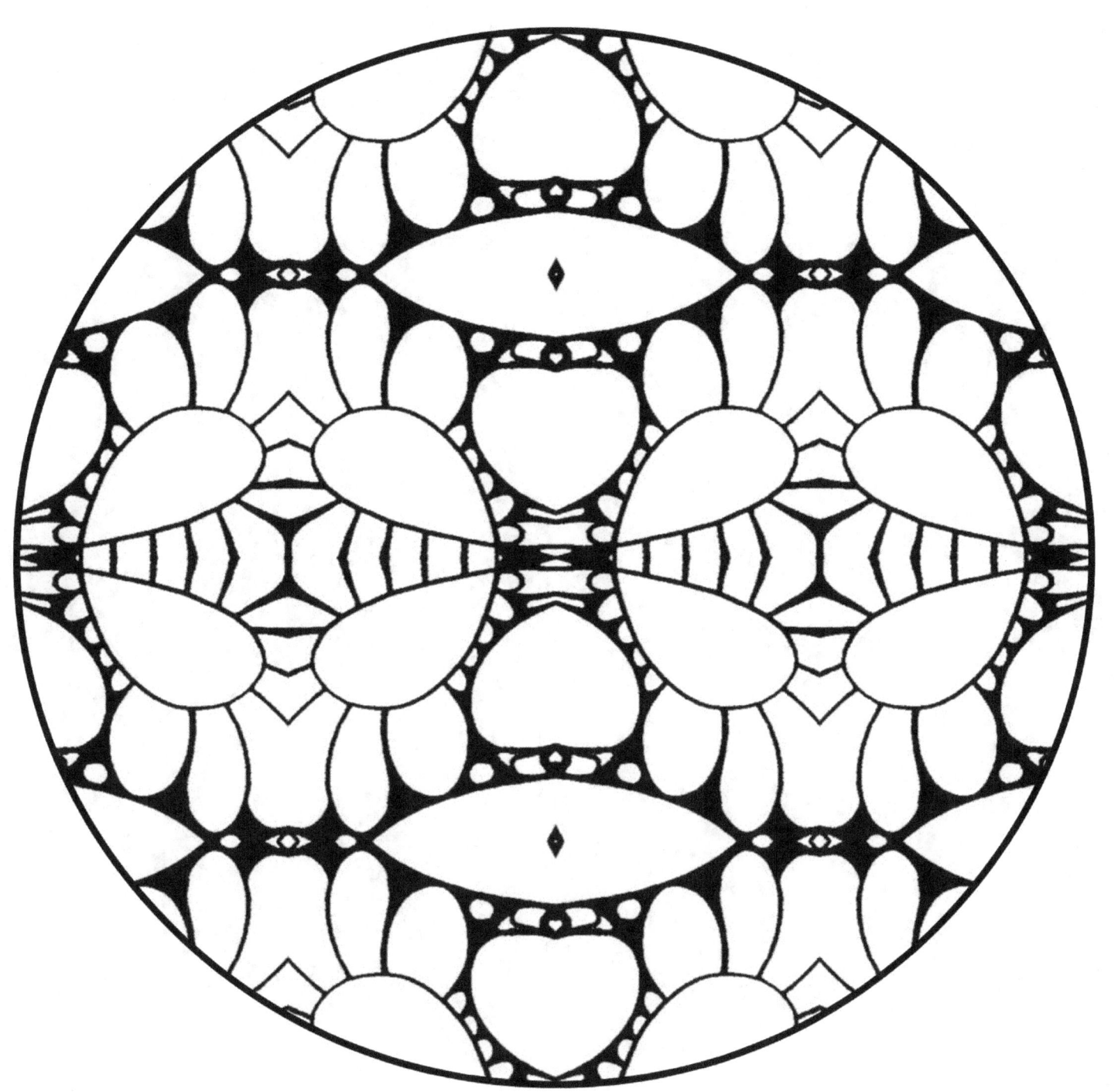